How to Discover the Motives of your Behaviour and the Secrets of Your Subconscious Mind

By
Mahmoud

Introduction

How can you discover how prepared you are for a life of improved psychological health, or how ready you are for a state of unrest, psychological turmoil, and instability in your everyday life?

Why do you become angry at someone without knowing the reason?

Why are you fearful of something, someone, or some event, confrontation, or entity without having a clear explanation?

Why do you feel anxious or nervous in certain situations without understanding the cause?

Why do you love one person and hate another, and why is it that when you confront yourself about it, you find no answer?

What are your greatest strengths and weaknesses?

In this book, you will discover the secrets behind the motives of your behaviour, and it will reveal the memories stored in your subconscious mind from the time you were a child until now.

In order to find the answers to all of your questions, simply follow these instructions, then send your feedback to the author:

info@ihossa.com

or

malmostshar@yahoo.com

If you wish to receive the file in Word format, please send us an email message and we will send it to you immediately.

After completing the application, you will receive the full analysis and a report containing the memories of your subconscious mind, and the secrets behind the motives of your behaviour.

Read each word carefully and individually, then record (either in writing or voice) the first thought that comes to your mind when you read the word. There are no right and wrong thoughts, neither are there any ethical nor unethical ones. The accuracy of the results depend on what exactly comes to your mind.

Word	Thought
Woman	

Milk	
Man	
Sun	
Moon	

Tree	
Deprivation	
Chicken	
Car	

Staircase	
Food	
Maid	

Boy	
Girl	

Country	
Fingers	

House

Ball

Eye	
Game	

Stomach	
Television	

Yesterday	
Bride	

School	
Night	

Cartoon	
Bed	

Room

Street

Dog	
Bicycle	

Cat	
Mirror	

Prayer	
Love	

Childhood	
Adolescence	

Sex	
Water	

Horse	
Me	

| Mouth | |
| Success | |

Failure	
Ice	

Tears	
Hand	

Forest	
Heart	

Obesity	
Slenderness	

Mother	
Wall	

Paper	
Fear	

Sorrow	
Anger	

Father	
Sister	

Brother	
Neighbours	

Adolescence	
Family	

Punishment	
Reward	

Smile	
Picture	

Beauty	
Unconscious	

urination	
Murder	
Blood	

Plane	
Car	

Red light	
Molesting	

Intimacy	
Assault	

Friend	
Girlfriend	

Pleasure	
Bird	

| Freedom | |

Affection	
Stubbornness	

	Pen
	Internet

Teacher	
Female	

teacher	
Possible	
Peak	

Kitchen	
Party	

Yellow

Red	
Black	

	Green	
	White	

Blue	
Tree	

Death	
Illness	

Anxiety	
Depression	

Door	
Poverty	

Wealth	
Darkness	

Sleep	
Day	

Week	
Month	

Year	
Rose	

Box	
Examination	

Study

In order to find the answers to all of your questions, simply follow these instructions, then send your feedback to the author:

info@ihossa.com

or

malmostshar@yahoo.com

If you wish to receive the file in Word format, please send us an email message and we will send it to you immediately.

After completing the application, you will receive the full analysis and a report containing the memories of your subconscious mind, and the secrets behind the motives of your behaviour.

For any enquiries, please contact us through these email addresses:

info@ihossa.com

or

malmostshar@yahoo.com